the
information
store
☎ 01603 773114
email: tis@ccn.

WEDNESDAY

Andy Croft

Published in association with The Basic Skills Agency

Hodder & Stoughton

A MEMBER OF THE HODDER HEADLINE GROUP

Acknowledgements

Cover: Darren Walsh/Action Images.

*Photos: p. 5 © Action-Plus photographers, London; pp. v, 19, 24 © Allsport, London;
pp. 8, 10 Action Images; pp. 14, 16 © Hulton Getty, London.*

Orders: please contact Bookpoint Ltd, 39 Milton Park, Abingdon, Oxon OX14 4TD. Telephone: (44)
01235 400414, Fax: (44) 01235 400454. Lines are open from 9.00–6.00, Monday to Saturday, with a
24 hour message answering service. Email address: orders@bookpoint.co.uk

British Library Cataloguing in Publication Data
A catalogue record for this title is available from The British Library

ISBN 0 340 74736 6

First published 1999
Impression number   10 9 8 7 6 5 4 3 2 1
Year   2004 2003 2002 2001 2000 1999

Typeset by Fakenham Photosetting Ltd, Fakenham, Norfolk.
Printed in Great Britain for Hodder & Stoughton Educational, a division of Hodder Headline Plc, 338
Euston Road, London NW1 3BH by Redwood Books, Trowbridge, Wiltshire.

Contents

Hillsborough, home of Sheffield Wednesday.

Wednesday are the fifth oldest club
in England.
They are Yorkshire's biggest club.
Their famous ground at Hillsborough
is one of the best in Britain.
They have won the FA Cup three times.
They have won the Championship four times –
but that was a long time ago.

Everyone still expects them to win.
No one is surprised when they don't.

Wednesday fans are used to things going wrong.
There's never a dull moment at Wednesday.

Sheffield Wednesday are like a sleeping giant.
One day they will wake up.

Then everyone will have to watch out.

1 Beginning

Sheffield Wednesday are a
world famous football club today.
However, they began life
over a hundred years ago
as a cricket club.
In those days people in Sheffield
had to work on Saturdays.
They could play cricket only
on Wednesday afternoons.
So they were called
the Wednesday Cricket Club.
In 1867 some of the cricketers
started a football team.
That is how Sheffield Wednesday
got their name.

2 Early Days

Wednesday have played in blue and white hoops.
They have played in blue and white squares.
They have played in blue shirts
with white sleeves.
Today they play in blue and white stripes.
They have always played in blue and white!

Wednesday did not join the Football League
when it started in 1888.
Instead they helped to set up
the Football Alliance.
A few years later
the Alliance joined the League.
This made two divisions.
Wednesday went straight into the top division.

In those days Wednesday used to play
at lots of different grounds.
They even played at Bramhall Lane
(now the home of Sheffield United).

Because Sheffield was famous
for making knives,
they used to be known as 'the Blades'
(now Sheffield United's nickname).
In 1899 the club moved to Owlerton.
That is why they are called 'the Owls'.
Today the club's mascots are Ollie Owl,
Ozzie Owl and Bazz (the owl with attitude).

The Owlerton ground
is now called Hillsborough.
It is one of the finest grounds in England.
FA Cup semi-finals have been played there
for nearly 90 years.

Four World Cup games were played
at Hillsborough in 1966.

One of Wednesday's club mascots.

But Hillsborough is also remembered for disaster.
In 1914 a wall collapsed,
injuring many fans.

The worst disaster was in 1989.
Liverpool and Notts Forest were playing
an FA Cup semi-final.
There was a very big crowd.
95 fans were crushed to death.
Another 170 were hurt.

3 Making History

In 1876 Wednesday bought a Scottish player
called James Lang.
He was the first 'foreigner'
to play in English football.
In those days it was against the rules
to pay footballers.
So a rich Wednesday fan
gave him a job in a local steelworks.

In 1886 Wednesday were not allowed
to play in the FA Cup.
Their application form did not arrive in time.

At that time clubs were only allowed
to give a new player £10 to sign on.
In 1893 Wednesday paid two players
£120 to sign for the club.
They were in trouble with the FA
for doing this.

Wednesday paid a record price for Paolo di Canio.
But in the old days, clubs were not allowed
to pay footballers.

In 1898 Wednesday were playing Aston Villa.
The referee was late for the match,
so the game started late.
Soon it got dark.
The players couldn't see the ball very well.

The referee blew for time.
But there were still 11 minutes to go.
Villa wanted to play the match again.
But Wednesday were winning 3–1.
They wanted to finish the match.
The FA agreed.

They made Wednesday and Villa finish the match
a few weeks later.
Three thousand people went to see them.
The match only lasted 11 minutes!
Wednesday scored again to win 4–1.
After this the FA said teams must play
all 90 minutes in future.

Chris Waddle claps the fans after a game.
Wednesday were the first team to run
a 'loser's' lap of honour.

In 1966 Wednesday lost 3–2 to Everton
in the FA Cup Final.
But they played very well.
After the match they ran a lap of honour
around the pitch.
They were the first losers to do this
at Wembley.

4 Winning

Wednesday have played in 16
FA Cup semi-finals.
A hundred years ago they reached
the quarter-finals every season for nine years.

Once they played on a pitch
that didn't have any goal posts.
Wednesday had to take their own posts
with them.

Wednesday have played in six FA Cup Finals.
They have won the cup three times.

In the 1896 Cup Final,
Wednesday beat Wolves 2–1.
Both Wednesday's goals were scored
by Fred Spoksley.
He hit one so hard it bounced
straight out again.
The Wolves keeper didn't even know
it had gone in!

In the 1907 final Wednesday beat Everton 2–1.
Their goals were scored by
Stewart and Simpson.

In 1935 Wednesday were in the Cup Final again.
Ellis Rimmer had scored for Wednesday
in every round.

At Wembley someone gave him
a lucky horse-shoe at half-time.
Wednesday beat West Brom 4–2,
with two late goals by Ellis Rimmer.

The 1935 Cup Final.
Wednesday beat West Brom 4–2.

5 Losing

By the 1950s Wednesday fans were getting used
to their club going up and down.
They were promoted four times
and relegated three times in nine years.

Wednesday's striker Derek Dooley
was the best centre-forward of his day.
He once scored 47 goals in 31 games.
Unfortunately he broke his leg playing
against Preston in 1953.
His leg did not get better.
In the end he lost his leg.

Derek Dooley scored 47 goals
in 31 games for Wednesday.

In 1965 three Wednesday players called
Tony Kay, Peter Swan and 'Bronco' Lane
were caught fixing matches.
They were banned from football for life.

By the 1970s Wednesday fans were getting used
to things going wrong.
They were getting used to going down.
They went into the Second Division.
Then they went into the Third Division.
They nearly went into the Fourth Division!
They were saved by just one point.

One fan was so upset he emigrated.
Another fan tried to sue the club.
He wanted his money back.
He said they played so badly
it wasn't really football.

They slowly climbed back to the top,
but in 1991 they went down again.

6 Winning Again

Under manager Big Ron Atkinson,
Wednesday bounced straight back
into the top flight.
And this time it looked like
they were going to stay.

That season they met Manchester United
in the Rumbelows Cup Final.
John Sheridan scored.
Wednesday won 1–0.
They brought the cup back to Sheffield.
Wednesday had won something at last!

After Ron Atkinson,
Wednesday had another new manager.
He was called Trevor Francis.
He was a brilliant midfield player.
He used to play for England.

Big Ron Atkinson,
the former Sheffield Wednesday manager
who helped the team bounce back.

The next season the Owls were really hooting.
They had a brilliant team.

Chris Woods was in goal.
Nigel Pearson and Carlton Palmer
were in defence.
David Hirst and Paul Warhurst
were in the attack.
Wednesday had not won the League
for 62 years,
but it looked as if the Championship
was coming back to Yorkshire at last.
It did.
But not to Sheffield.
On the last day of the season
Wednesday lost the title to Leeds!

Trevor Francis was determined
to win something for Wednesday.
In 1993 they reached the final
of the Coca-Cola Cup.
They were beaten 2–1 by Arsenal.
That year they also reached the FA Cup Final.
Guess who they had to play?
Arsenal!
David Hirst scored for Wednesday.
They drew 1–1 at Wembley.
In the replay Chris Waddle scored for Wednesday.
But they lost the replay – 2–1 again.

7 Losing Again

By 1995 Wednesday had another new manager.
He was called David Pleat.
He built a new team.
He bought Paulo di Canio from Celtic.
He bought Benito Carbone for £3 million.
Wednesday played very exciting football.

At the start of 1997 everyone expected
Wednesday to do well.
But they didn't.
They were beaten 7–2 by Blackburn.
They were beaten 6–1 by Manchester United.
By November they had only nine points
from 13 games.
David Pleat was sacked.

Big Ron Atkinson came back
to save his old club.
No one thought he could do it.
But he did.
They avoided relegation.
Just.

Joy for Sheffield Wednesday
as they beat Spurs 3–0 at White Hart Lane.

8 Winning Again?

Now Wednesday have another new manager.
His name is Danny Wilson.
Danny Wilson used to play for Wednesday.
He took Barnsley into the Premiership.
Who knows –
he may bring the glory days
back to Wednesday.

Wednesday fans hope so.
Ollie, Ozzie and Bazz hope so.
And so do the players.
Brilliant players like:
Kevin Pressman
Benito Carbone
Mark Pembridge
Andy Booth
Andy Hinchcliffe
Paulo di Canio

Perhaps the sleeping giant
of English football
is about to wake up at last …

If you have enjoyed this book, you may like to read other books in the *Livewire* series.

Blackburn Rovers
Derby County
Leeds United
West Ham United
Arsenal
Manchester United